Experimental
Primate

Selected Poems

EXPERIMENTAL

PRIMATE

SELECTED POEMS

Sue Flaster

ASPHODEL PRESS

Kingston, Rhode Island & Lancaster, England

Published by Asphodel Press
Copyright © 2011 by Sue Flaster

First Printing, 2011

LIBRARY OF CONGRESS
CATALOGING-IN-PUBLICATION DATA

Sue Flaster, 1943-
Experimental primate

p. 66   cm. 21.5
I. Title   2011
C.I.P. available upon request   2011-999999
from the Library of Congress   CIP
ISBN: 1-55921-999-1 (paperbound : alk. paper)

Acknowledgments

With deepest thanks to Britt Bell,
who never hesitated.

Printed in the United States of America
Distributed in North America by Midpoint Trade Books
27 West 20th street #1102
NY, NY 10011
(212) 727-0190, midpointtradebooks.com

in the United Kingdom, Eire, and Europe by
Gazelle Book Services Ltd.,
White Cross Mills, High Town,
Lancaster LA1 1RN England,
1-44-1524-68765, gazellebooks.co.uk

For Harald

CONTENTS

EXPERIMENTAL PRIMATE

THE RECORDED VOICE
OF JUSSI BJÖRLING

The recorded voice of Jussi Björling
(without which this is neither possible
nor necessary)
shimmers
as I split the hairs of small emotions.

I've foolishly declared
I want a man
who's built himself a nest
of newsprint.
A person should know better:
bad memories have the half-life
of the planet;
the half-life of despairing
can't be measured.

I offer to unhinge his life:
dramatic gesture
is so flattering and easy;
the daily compromise
of bed and bath
demands a different fortitude
I've never learned.

There are other singers,
not that it matters.
This voice is all of everything

we need.
His secret song of triumph
brings us back,
together,
and to him.

FOGGY MORNINGS

Some foggy mornings
late-rising deer look up
as the commuter bus goes by.

Only the tops of mountains
are dark against the sky.
The damp breath of the place
comes out of the earth
and into our bones.

Some mornings,
I can barely stand——
the look of the sky
can pin me
to my pillow.
You roll over
and face me——
the news of your warmth arrives
a moment before your touch.

1939 LUCERNE VERDI "REQUIEM"

The recorded voice of Jussi Björling
(without which this is neither
possible nor necessary)
glides out of static
like wind over water,
disembodied, substantial,
a tender trumpet:
he and Toscanini
find God
in an armed forces
radio broadcast.

LONG FLIGHT

Two months without you,
five days of strangling every feeling
(mostly irritation,
the appendix of childhood,
old days when I was bullied),
and finally we're flying.

I have no assignment here,
baggage in a chair
a little cramped,
belongings out of reach.

And then I feel you, see you,
smell you,
taste
a wave of you,
a wind,
a bath
of you.
I struggle not to weep,
back here in coach.

WHAT KIND OF TRIBUTE

What kind of tribute
can I send you:
our first fruits and acorns
and our laughter
burn on this fire,
their honeyed smoke
rising.
What can we send you:
echoes of our conversation
rise with the smoke
of our laughter.
No one here
waits for an answer.

What kind of tribute
can I send you,
where you are?

SLEEPING MAN

I like to watch you sleep.
It's new to me,
this interest in your breathing.
The changes in your face
as dreams begin and end
are so much like the twitches of surprise
you've never learned to hide
when something pleases you.

Your stillness floors me.
Such a difference from the daylight man
whose long loose bones are tossed about;
I wonder—sometimes—how you balance
long enough
to walk.

IT DOESN'T MATTER

It doesn't matter
how you spell the name—
the dead don't read well,
but always hear their names aloud:
they wait for us to call them.
What can they tell us?

From the silence in between
the beats of blood,
they speak, they sing,
they remember
a hoarse voice,
a strange bed,
the taste of morning.

ONE MORE FUTURE DISAPPEARING

One more future disappearing
doesn't give the others substance.
You who see me slowly fading
are not liable to renewal
at this dissolution sell-out:
I am going out of business.

Impermanent reminders of
capriciousness and change—
one more failure of prediction
doesn't raise the cost of
omen-reading. Artifice
is here to stay.

DATES

My lover (Mr. Tall Guy) eats
the dates I send him with such self-restraint
it makes me dizzy.

It isn't out of meanness, I've decided.
He offers them to other, gripped between
a pair of tiny tongs,
presented with delight,
a pleasure to be shared.

Alone, he clatters through the dark
and eats a single date,
held in the same tongs.

My lover walks upstairs,
the sweet and grainy memory
of dates
is melting,
as he climbs.

THINGS HIDE

Things hide themselves.
It's true:
a favorite pen,
the desire to be touched,
canter away,
and the Sun of our planets
can't reach into the corners
where they lie,
a little dusty,
in the leavings of spiders,
paper clips,
scraps of music.

They wait for the right moment
to reappear;
slightly superior,
got tears on their faces
like hungry children.
Crouched in the corner,
trembling like orphans,
breathless for a groping hand
to reach around the chair legs
and touch them,
missing so long,
so recently remembered,

they lose patience with us,
curse our dullness;
wonder why it took so long
to miss them.

DOLPHIN DAY

In the afternoon
I walk down to the waterfront.
Dolphins wash in
with the tide.
They don't do much—
a grey head
stays above the ruffles
searching for bubbles,
other signs of the things
that please them.

I swam with them, once,
in the Bahamas.
We were in the water with them,
up to our necks.
I was frightened at first:
they look very big and fast when
you're treading water.
A female went around me
2 or 3 times,
and then pressed herself
against my back.

"They want to hear your heart beat,
if they like you," said the keeper.

How nice to know
their likes and dislikes
arrive in the same way as ours.
I could feel her heart,
as well.

ETNA

That mountain disappears at night.
Two lights hang over the vanished slopes
and its fires burn alone
over the sea.
Villages turn their balconies
to the light.

In the sulphur and steam
of the newest fire,
above the blackness of the mountain's children,
I lose you in the rising rain,
floating in the mountain's thunder.

The morning beach was brighter than a dream,
the sky and water paralyzed with heat,
and then the solid water fell—
deranged exaggeration of the rain—
crippled birds were falling at our feet,
the waves lay flattened on the shore.
Noon Sun dried the battered town,
and a mad old man was singing on the road.

Beautiful mountain, they call it.
We drove up the black road
between scrawls of white paint:

the names of bicycle racers.
Fading villages bleached inside
their stony black wind-breaks—
squares on the mountain of grapes,
their blue-eyed faces cracked and dry.

Rolling from fire
the wind and its cargo
have covered our mouths with dust.
The primitive echoes of thunder and faith
deliver our faces from speech.
I follow you over the loose light rock
through the sulphurous fog,
past the crater.

SURPRISES

There's no shortage
of surprises here.
The answers don't reveal themselves
in tidy declarations
cut from some familiar grammar.

I've never felt so far adrift.
You seem untroubled,
revising your revisions.
Caught for a moment between the bookcase
and the desk,
you can spare a warm word and a smile
without breaking stride.

Over here on the couch,
all I can do is chew my lip
and wonder what comes next.

MOUNTAINS BELONG
TO THE WINTER

Mountains belong to the winter,
their season of invisibility.
The white sky has no horizons,
snow and clouds
settle in the same density,
compact, unbounded and still.
Look up through the window.
Separateness ends in the paint spots
left on the glass: it is all one mass.
Look up through the window.
The featureless air is opaque
as the mountains. The mountains
are part of the clouds.
There is no more transparency,
no more reflection.
The spaces are filled up.
The world is abridged
in the mass of the air.
The earth is contained
in the bowl of the mountains,
filled to the crest with the whiteness
of light without shadow.
Look up through the window.
The creatures of light have appeared.
They are swimming in mountains,
in monochrome oceans of air.

ON GROWING OLD

On growing old, philanderer,
the blood does not,
predictably,
run cold,
but only cannot make
the flesh so warm.

NOTES ON THE PLACEMENT
OF MY RIGHT HAND

I can think of eleven or twelve quite current reasons
why I should walk up to you and just plain and
simply

      goose you as hard as I can.

By the way, and as long as we're on the subject,
      (you've probably noticed)
you also rather fascinate me in other ways,
but basically,
first things first.

WORLD'S SMALLEST DALA HORSE

(note: the Dala horse is the wooden painted symbol of
the Swedish province of Dalarna—-Dalecarlia. They
range in size from 60 meters high to nearly invisible)

Some ants were walking on a fine new road
through gravel,
undistracted, weightless nearly,
shifting stone one atom at a time,
I guess,
to excavate the perfect
two-way street;
striking out for dinner,
strutting home with parcels,
balancing their diets
as they travel.

I prefer to be inspired, in general.
Those ants embarrass some old sense
of what's an obligation,
duty,
grown-up willingness
to do the job.

The world's smallest carved and painted horse
is just a speck.
It's in the Book of Records
where it proves
that ants

are not the only ones
who labor
on a sub-atomic scale.

This speck could be the king's new clothes,
but I can see the painted saddle
with a naked eye.
The sculptor (who's enormous)
worked three hours
with a sharpened whisker,
gave up coffee,
made himself a miracle
of stillness
while he shaped it.

Things he makes in human scale——
pictures, cupboards—
look like secrets,
bad dreams,
memories of other planets.

This tiny horse announces:
times have changed.
The work is good,
and stillness is the prize.

SURVIVOR SYNDROME

This was the year
when I had to explain
to orderlies and
cemetery gardeners
that I was neither an ambulance chaser
nor a professional mourner.

The nurses were curiously
concerned for my posture.
They kept still and watched
as I wedged myself into
the corner smoker
to survey the place,
ignoring perspective
like a primitive.
Coy physicians
made their morning over-flights
and disappeared;
aunts and second cousins
clustered in the halls
and sped away
in blood-tied order;
I was bound there
by some strange abstraction
of duty or affection,
and clearly excluded
from medical or relative identity:

45

a foreign body
afloat in a hallway
as flat as a postcard.

This was the year when
I learned to see the faces
in the high white beds;
got used to tubes and bottles
(finally, I did):
accepted the body
in the middle of the plumbing
as if it had never lived alone,
which is treason,
but the bodies were so many.

Old jokes and drinking habits
get shuttled off to history.
The dust of probability
sits on the stainless-steel.
Premature past-tense
pops into the room
like the wrong end of a telescope,
and long before reality recedes,
recognition concedes defeat.
I incredibly survive,
at odd moments remembering
how simple last week was,
before your unexpected self
was added to the list of
this year's dead and dying.

AUGUST

This Swedish Sun
is mild and warm;
the pale-eyed locals
have gathered in the square
to bask and listen to musicians
from the old-age home.

I miss the mid-day heat,
Sun making my bones sweat
and soften,
the easy walk of loose shoulders.
A slice of shade at Noon
can make me cross the street.

It's so quiet here.
The afternoon bus home
was full of high school kids.
Their purple hair and piercings
made me feel less need
to start a fight
with you.

We're so alike.
These practiced solitudes
are what we've built
instead of compromise;

a single bed is such a statement
of intent.

What are you like
when you're angry?
Is this the moment you've been
waiting for,
to take your freedom
and your silence back,
to find your dishes
where you left them,
walk at your own pace
to the bus stop?
tears are such a mystery;
a bad day makes us both so fragile——
history is always living
when you reach our age.
The old offenses, given and received,
can mobilize themselves
and go right for the throat
unless we take a stand here
and agree that we are not
our mothers, fathers, husbands, children.
It was just a bad day
and it's over.

EXPERIMENTAL PRIMATE

I am an experimental primate,
feeling my way through a maze
full of knobs and door sills.
My hand shakes over the hot water faucet.
I am patiently disposed around the pipes
which reach up from the floor
and disappear
behind the neatly plastered holes
above me.

I am a defrocked tree climber,
rubbing my nails in the
ragged cracks
that hold the tiles together on the wall.
I walked to the kitchen this morning
and found my eye-level
surprisingly higher
than what I recalled.
The wall goes on above the tiles;
there is a light switch
and an English calendar with photographs
of unknown playwrights' country houses.

I am a shaky grub-eater,
bumping through this turning

full of objects built to hold me.
I can stand on my hind legs
and change the months.
I am even more improbable
than the cottage belonging
to Mrs. Alec Beesley.

BUREAU OF THE BUDGET BLUES

.

When you wake up in the morning
don't be angry, don't be hurt
if I have left you---
I'm living on credit.
The time I had for wasting
has all been ticked away,
the bureau of the budget blues.

In the middle of the morning
read the paper, drink your coffee,
pull the curtains---
don't listen for the doorbell.
My capitol is tiny
and I'm spending every day,
the bureau of the budget blues

When I walk around the corner,
just can't help it, I keep looking at your windows,
but please don't expect me.
I'm running out the hours,
I can't stop along the way,
the bureau of the budget blues.

VERY LATE AUGUST

So many memories,
useless, harmless,
cram the fragile box
between my shoulders:
illicit cigarettes
and dormitory drama,
an English film about
two gangster brothers.

And then
we rang the dean's doorbell one night.
She invited us for tea
and made me pour:
my discomfort
payment
for our unannounced appearance.

My own father,
poor man,
struggled to be seen
above the middle.
Lived the middle well
and full of rage.
His face, in pictures,
always stone,
but I remember
drunken parties without guilt,

many friends,
silly hats.

I haven't learned
to measure effort---
perhaps I won't,
at this late date.
Every trip means
pictures, plates,
on every surface;
I don't know:
it seems to make a nest
for no one.

My brother doesn't want the house,
my past,
he'll pack it all in bags
for pick-up
on the Monday run,
and I don't blame him.
Who else could care
about these things,
reminders of what I
remember,
soon to seem too much
for any other.

It's just a fact, after all:
we don't last,
nothing lasts:

my Stanglware
will find a home at Habitat,
old photos (never sorted)
meet their rightful fate,
some objects will reach friends
or brothers,
most will find the same way
as what's in my head,
and that seems fair
to me.

COLOPHON

Sue Flaster attended Douglass College
a long time ago. She worked in publishing
sales, book distribution and wholesaling for
nearly 30 years. Sue and her husband commute
between Charleston, South Carolina and
Säter in the Swedish province of Dalarna.
She runs, reads and talks a lot, and currently
serves on the Board of the Jussi Björling
Society-USA.

The text was set in Centaur, a typeface designed
by Bruce Rogers (1870-1957). Considered the
finest American designer of the last century,
Rogers designed this face in 1914 for the
Montague Press edition of *The Centaur* by
Maurice Guerin. Centaur was first available to
the printing trade in 1929 from Monotype.
Roger's masterpiece of design using Centaur was
the *Oxford Lectern Bible* published in 1935.
Sabon was used for the pagination. The display
faces are BankGothic and Trajan.

This book was typeset by Rhode Island Book
Composition, Kingston, Rhode Island and
printed by Gasch Printing of Odenton,
Maryland on acid free paper.